WITHDRAWN

MY STATE! ★

Tennessee

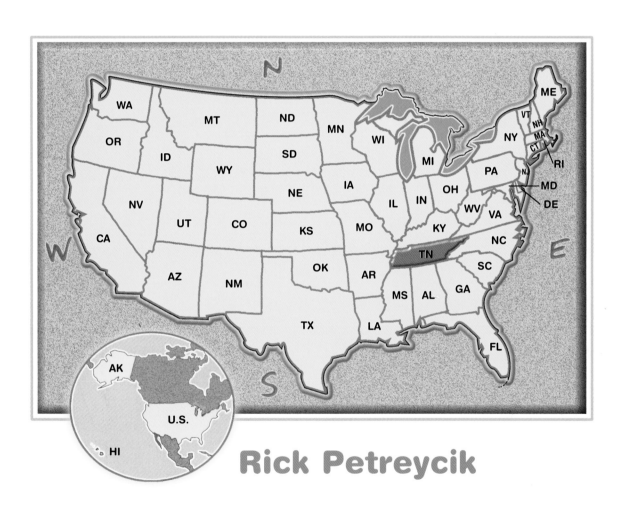

Rick Petreycik

Marshall Cavendish
Benchmark
New York

Marshall Cavendish Benchmark
99 White Plains Road
Tarrytown, New York 10591-9001
www.marshallcavendish.us

Library of Congress Cataloging-in-Publication Data

Petreycik, Rick.
Tennessee / by Rick Petreycik.
p. cm. — (It's my state!)
Summary: "Surveys the history, geography, economy, and people of
Tennessee"—Provided by publisher.
Includes bibliographical references and index.
ISBN 0-7614-1909-8
1. Tennessee—Juvenile literature. I. Title. II. Series.

F436.3.P48 2006
976.8—dc22
2005018057

Photo research by Candlepants Incorporated

Cover photograph: Morris Abernathy/Corbis
Back cover illustration: The license plate shows Tennessee's postal abbreviation followed by its year of statehood.

Series design by Anahid Hamparian

Printed in Malaysia

1 3 5 6 4 2

Contents

A Quick Look at Tennessee

Nickname: The Volunteer State

Population: 5,900,962 (2004 estimate)

Statehood: June 1, 1796

Tree: Tulip Poplar

Many of the early settlers of Tennessee made their houses, barns, and places of business out of tulip poplar. The tree's bark is smooth and brownish gray, and its flowers look like green-orange tulips. The tulip poplar was made the official state tree in 1947.

Bird: Mockingbird

This grayish-white bird makes its home throughout Tennessee. The bird is well known for its beautiful singing voice. It also imitates the songs of other birds, which is why it is called the mockingbird. The mockingbird became Tennessee's state bird in 1933.

Wildflower: Passionflower

The passionflower is Tennessee's official wildflower. This striking flower can be found in a variety of colors. Sometimes a passionflower is called a may-pop, a wild apricot, or an ocoee. The passionflower was first made the state flower in 1919. The state later chose the iris as the state cultivated flower, and in 1973 made the passionflower the official wildflower.

4

Wild Animal: Raccoon

In 1971, the Tennessee General Assembly adopted the raccoon as the official state wild animal. The raccoon is a furry mammal that is easily recognized by its striped, bushy tail and the black masklike band around its eyes. In the wild, raccoons eat berries, nuts, insects, small birds and their eggs, and small animals such as frogs and fish. Raccoons are wild animals, but they can often be seen around neighborhoods and homes—eating from birdfeeders, gardens, and even garbage cans.

Gem: Freshwater Pearl

Tennessee's freshwater rivers contain mussels, which are aquatic animals similar to oysters. Mussels are often harvested for food. They also make shiny freshwater pearls, which come in a variety of shapes and colors.

Insects: Firefly and Ladybug

Tennessee has two state insects: the firefly and the ladybug. The firefly produces a glow-in-the-dark light that makes it easy to spot on summer evenings. The reddish-orange ladybug is a type of beetle with little black spots on its wings. Farmers especially like ladybugs because they feed on insects that harm crops.

1 The Volunteer State

Tennessee is a state with a natural landscape that is full of variety. It has dense forests, breathtaking mountains, scenic valleys, and rolling rivers. Tennessee lies in a region that is popularly called the Upper South. Other states in the Upper South include Virginia, North Carolina, and Arkansas.

Tennessee sort of resembles a huge rectangle. It lies between the Mississippi River on the west and the Appalachian Mountains on the east. Its distance from east to west is approximately 491 miles. From north to south the state stretches 115 miles. Tennessee's total area makes it the thirty-sixth-largest state in the country.

Tennessee's Borders

North: Kentucky and Virginia
South: Mississippi, Alabama, and Georgia
East: North Carolina
West: Arkansas, Missouri, and the Mississippi River

Because of the location of its mountains, rivers, and lowlands, Tennessee can be divided into three regions. They are East Tennessee, Middle Tennessee, and West Tennessee.

East Tennessee

East Tennessee is a very mountainous region. The Appalachian Mountains, which extend all the way from Maine to central Alabama, form Tennessee's eastern border. Among the Appalachian ranges that can be seen in East Tennessee are the Chilhowees, Snowbirds, Unakas, and Great Smokies. The Great Smokies were given their name because of a bluish-gray haze that seems to hover around their peaks. Clingman's Dome is found within Tennessee's Great Smoky Mountains National Park. At 6,643 feet, it is Tennessee's highest peak.

The Appalachian ridges offer visitors a breathtaking view in Great Smoky Mountains National Park.

But the region is not all mountains. There are many wooded and wilderness areas, as well as a few small communities. One of Tennessee's large cities is almost 40 miles northwest of Clingman's Dome. Knoxville served as Tennessee's first capital.

Great Smoky Mountains National Park, which opened to the public in 1940, has plenty of scenic forests, waterfalls, and meadows. The park is the most frequently visited national park in the United States. Around nine million visitors pass through it each year.

To the west of the Appalachians is a high, fertile, wooded area with flat-topped mountains that range in elevation from 1,500 to 1,800 feet. This area also contains a large number of streams. Over the years, the water's constant flowing motion helped create deep, V-shaped valleys. This section of the state lies in the Cumberland Plateau, which extends northward from Alabama to Kentucky. (A plateau is a portion of flat land that has been raised higher than the surrounding land.) Chattanooga, Tennessee's fourth-largest city, is located in this region.

The Ocoee River, located in southeastern Tennessee, has been rated one of the best white-water recreational rivers in the United States. Because of that, it was chosen as the site for the white water canoe/kayak competition during the 1996 Summer Olympics.

Located in the Cumberland Plateau, Chattanooga is a thriving city.

Middle Tennessee

Middle Tennessee's natural landscape is shaped like a deep bowl. The outer edge of this bowl is known as the Highland Rim. The rim has steep mountain slopes made mostly of limestone. Beneath the surface of the rim are a number of hollowed out caves and underground streams.

The area within the bowl is known as the Nashville Basin. Covering more than 6,450 square miles, the Nashville Basin is a mostly flat region that has some of the richest farmland in the state. Its soil is perfect for farming. Many crops that have been produced in this region over the years include wheat, potatoes, tomatoes, tobacco, and fruit trees.

Because of the soil's high concentration of limestone, which contains nutrients, the Nashville Basin is also perfect pastureland. Grasses grow well here and as a result, plenty of beef and dairy cattle, sheep, and horses have been raised in Middle Tennessee, where they can graze—or eat—well.

Middle Tennessee's major cities include Clarksville and Nashville, which is Tennessee's capital and second-largest city. Many smaller cities and towns are located near these larger cities. This region of Tennessee has the state's largest populations.

Livestock such as horses graze on the rich grasses that grow in Middle Tennessee's fertile soil.

West Tennessee

West Tennessee is made up of low, fertile flatlands that are occasionally broken up by rolling hills, valleys, and streams. The Tennessee River cuts through part of West Tennessee. Cities and towns lie along the banks of this large river.

> Tennessee's name is believed to come from the word *Tanasi*. This is the name the Cherokee people gave villages that were located near the river we now call the Tennessee River.

The far western corner of the region has the best farmland in the state. That is because the Mississippi River, which forms Tennessee's western border, carries silt—a collection of sand clay, dirt, and other minerals that enrich the soil—and deposits it along the surrounding banks. Cotton, soybeans, and timber are just some of the many agricultural products that spring from the nutrient-rich soil in this region.

Reelfoot Lake, Tennessee's largest natural lake, is located in the northwestern section of West Tennessee. How Reelfoot Lake was shaped is an interesting story. Between December 16, 1811 and March 15, 1812, a series of earthquakes and their aftershocks rocked the area where Missouri, Kentucky, and Tennessee meet. The quakes were so severe that they caused the Mississippi

Bald cypress trees grow out from within Reelfoot Lake. Some of these trees took root in the soil before the land became covered with water.

River to change its course and set a huge wave into motion. The wave was so big and powerful that it left behind a lake where there once had been cypress, walnut, and cottonwood trees.

West Tennessee is also the home of Memphis, Tennessee's largest city. Lying on the Mississippi River in the far southwestern corner of the state, Memphis is Tennessee's center of cotton trading and hardwood manufacturing. It is also the home of music called the blues, as well as the birthplace of rock 'n' roll.

Memphis, which was founded in 1819, was named after an ancient Egyptian city located on the Nile River. Because people at the time compared the Mississippi River to the Nile, they named Tennessee's important port city after the Egyptian city of Memphis.

Besides being a highly traveled port city and trading center, Memphis also played an important part in the state's—and the nation's—music history.

Climate

Tennessee's climate varies from region to region. For example, West Tennessee's summer climate tends to be humid and warm. Average summer temperatures there hover above 80 degrees Fahrenheit, while in East Tennessee, the temperature is around 71 degrees. Winters in West Tennessee are generally mild, too, with temperatures approaching 50 degrees Fahrenheit.

By contrast, the average January temperature in East Tennessee is a chilly 37 degrees Fahrenheit. Snowfall and temperatures below zero are also quite common in East Tennessee during the winter months.

East Tennessee's average yearly snowfall is 12 inches, while 6 inches typically fall in West Tennessee. The state's average annual precipitation—which is a combination of rain, snow, and sleet—is 52 inches.

Despite its relatively mild year-round climate, Tennessee has experienced some extreme weather conditions throughout its history. The state's lowest temperature occurred in Mountain View on December 30, 1917, when the mercury dropped to a numbing minus 32 degrees. A record high was hit during the summer of 1930 in Perryville, when temperatures soared to 113 degrees on both July 29 and August 9.

Snow covers a street in Jonesboro, the oldest town in Tennessee.

Weather events that Tennesseans have learned to pay close attention to are flooding conditions and tornadoes. Flooding conditions come from heavy rains that usually fall in March and April, causing the state's rivers to overflow. The Mississippi River Flood of 1937 devastated a large portion of West Tennessee and left many people homeless. It was the worst flood in Tennessee history.

Tornadoes have become very common in the state. Through the years, the strength of the tornadoes has caused millions of dollars worth of damage to the state. But residents know to expect them and most people brace themselves for the powerful twisters. Tornado season usually runs from March through August, although tornadoes can occur any time of year.

Wild Life

When it comes to the great outdoors, Tennessee is a natural paradise. Half of the state is covered in forests, which are home to at least 150 different native trees. In East Tennessee's wooded areas, one can find trees such as basswood and buckeye. Evergreen trees such as hemlock, spruce, white pine, and southern balsam also thrive in eastern Tennessee.

A fast-moving stream cascades down mossy rocks in a Tennessee forest. Forests setting such as these provide homes for a variety of plants and animals in the state.

East Tennessee's plentiful hardwood trees include maple, cherry, yellow poplar, and several species of oak. In Middle Tennessee, red cedars populate the Highland Rim, while sweet gum, sycamore, and scrub oak can be found within the Nashville Basin. West Tennessee's fertile soil is the perfect growing spot for bald cypress, cottonwood, tupelo gum, water oak, pecan, swamp locust, and catalpa.

Many types of wildflowers brighten Tennessee's woods and fields. These include passionflowers, dragonroot, hop clovers, azaleas, holly, mountain laurels, and rhododendron. Saxifrage, hepaticas, bloodroot, wild honeysuckle, daisies, black-eyed Susans, wild asters, and violet blossoms also bloom across the state.

In addition to the plant life, more than eighty-one species of mammals inhabit Tennessee's many woodland areas. These include black bear, deer, rabbits, raccoons, skunks, beavers, muskrats, bobcats, flying squirrels, and red and gray foxes. In some of the mountainous areas, one can even find European wild boar, also known as razorbacks. It is believed they entered the Tennessee wild in 1920 after escaping from a game preserve in North Carolina.

More than 300 species of birds either make their home in Tennessee or pass through the state on their way to migration destinations. Among these feathered creatures are mocking-birds, cardinals, robins, eastern bluebirds, wood thrushes, eastern towhee, and Carolina wrens. Rare golden eagles have been seen in Tennessee's Great Smoky Mountains. Among the eye-catching birds that nest along the state's many rivers are egrets and herons. Game birds such as ducks, geese, and quail are nearly everywhere, too. Wild turkeys can be spotted in remote parts of the eastern mountains.

Many fish and shellfish make their homes within Tennessee's rivers—and also within its lakes and streams. These include trout, mussels, catfish, saugers, black bass, walleyes, bluegills, bream, and white bass. However, certain fish, such as the bluemask darter and pallid sturgeon, have been placed on the state's endangered species list because their populations are very low. Scientists believe that this has happened because much of the fish's natural habitat has been destroyed. To try to fix this, the U.S. Fish and Wildlife Service has put protection programs in place to help save these fish. These programs include using existing laws to protect the species and working with local landowners to preserve and protect the surrounding habitat.

Other endangered species in Tennessee include the Carolina northern flying squirrel, red wolf, red-cockaded woodpecker,

peregrine falcon, and whooping crane. Although not a native bird, the whooping crane stops in Tennessee as part of a 1,250-mile migration from Wisconsin to Florida's Gulf Coast. In 2001 some Tennessee residents participated in a very successful 140-mile walk-a-thon that raised much needed money to help preserve the endangered bird.

Northern flying squirrels make their homes in some of Tennessee's forests. The squirrels do not really fly. Instead, they glide from tree to tree, using stretched out skin flaps to keep them in the air.

A golden eagle perches on a boulder. These majestic birds can be seen gliding through the blue Tennessee skies.

Plants & Animals

Black Bear

This medium-sized bear is usually black or dark brown. It has small eyes, rounded ears, and five strong claws on each paw. Black bears like to eat nuts, berries, fruits, acorns, and plant roots. In Tennessee, black bears make their homes in many of the state's forests, and especially in the Great Smoky Mountains National Park.

Bobcat

The bobcat is a member of the cat family and has a white tip on its short tail. The animal has thick reddish-yellow brown fur, long legs, and short clusters of hair stemming from each of its ears. Small populations of bobcats live in eastern Tennessee, where they eat rabbits, rodents, birds, bats, and sometimes deer.

Woodchuck

The woodchuck, which is also known as the groundhog, is a gray-ish-brown animal. It has a small nose, short ears, and a bushy tail. Woodchucks dig their own homes—called burrows—which can have as many as five different entrances. Woodchucks eat grasses, clover, alfalfa, wheat, corn, soybeans, berries, and—unfortunately for many Tennessee gardeners—different types of flowers.

European Wild Boar

Occasionally seen in Tennessee's Great Smoky Mountains National Park, the European wild boar—or wild hog—tends to look for food in the evenings during the warm summer months. Its diet consists of leaves, stems, roots, beetles, caterpillars, earthworms, and crayfish. The European wild boar is sometimes called a razorback.

Mountain Laurel

The mountain laurel has deep pink and white flowers and leaves that are a shiny dark green. It reaches a maximum height of just under 3 feet. Though its name suggests that it is only found in the mountains, these plants grow in swamps and in other places with moist soils.

Azalea

Found along Tennessee's rocky slopes and woods, the azalea has narrow green leaves and pink, white, or orange flowers. The azalea's attractive blossoms usually bloom in May and June. The Tennessee climate is good for growing azaleas, and many residents plant them in their gardens.

2 From the Beginning

Archaeologists—people who study materials from past cultures—estimate that humans first entered Tennessee around 11,000 BCE. These people, who were the ancestors of Native Americans, were hunters and gatherers who moved around from place to place in small groups. Some of the caves along the banks of the region's rivers reveal blackened, charred walls where these people once built fires and cooked their meals.

About 2,500 years ago, the Native Americans began to plant corn and beans. They also wove blankets and made pottery bowls and specialized tools for planting, hunting, and eating. These early people also built large mounds that rose above the ground. Historians believe these mounds were used as burial grounds and contain the remains of some of these people, as well as some of their artifacts. The most famous of these burial sites are the Pinson Mounds, which are located near the town of Jackson in western Tennessee. These early people are often referred to as the Mound Builders. But the Mound Builders mysteriously disappeared by the end of the sixteenth century.

In 1926, this group of young Tennesseans poses for a photograph outside their log schoolhouse in Reliance.

Saul's Mound, which is more than 70 feet high, is one of the Pinson Mounds in Madison County.

Three other Native American groups, however, began to arrive and settle in the region—the Cherokee, the Creek, and the Chickasaw. The Cherokee inhabited the northern part of what is now known as East and Middle Tennessee. The Creek settled in the southeastern area. The Chickasaw favored the flatlands of western Tennessee.

All three groups lived in villages and planted squash, corn, and beans. They also gathered wild nuts and berries, fished in the region's rivers and streams, and hunted deer and wild turkey in the wooded areas. These Native Americans also had similar dwellings. In winter, several families shared a large rectangular house made of logs. During the summer months, they lived in houses made of trees woven together and plastered with mud.

Europeans Arrive
The first Europeans to enter the region were Spanish explorers under the leadership of Hernando De Soto. Between 1540 and

1541, De Soto and his men were looking for gold, which they never found. During their travels in the region, De Soto and his men mistreated the Natives Americans they encountered. They also left behind many diseases that were common among Europeans, but foreign to the Native people. These diseases included smallpox, measles, and diphtheria. The illnesses eventually spread from village to village, and many Native Americans died.

More than a century passed before Europeans appeared in the area of present-day Tennessee again. In the summer of 1673, two Englishmen entered the region. Their names were James Needham and Gabriel Arthur, and they both worked for Abraham Wood, a businessman from the English colony of Virginia. Wood was interested in developing a fur trade beyond the mountains of Virginia, so he asked Needham and Arthur to explore the area. While they were in the region, however, a band of Cherokee captured them. They killed Needham but spared Arthur.

For the next year, Arthur lived with the Cherokee people and learned how they hunted, planted, and fished. Eventually, he made his way into the colony of North Carolina, and when he did, he

Before the European settlers took control of most of the land, Tennessee's early Native Americans were able to freely practice their traditions.

told fellow colonists about his time with the Cherokee. He described the rivers and forests, which were full of beaver, mink, otter, and other furry animals. The pelts—or skin and fur—of these animals could be turned into expensive coats and other accessories. Within a year, trappers and hunters began crossing the mountains of Virginia and North Carolina to hunt in the land that would become Tennessee.

France also began to turn its eyes toward this area. In 1682 a French explorer named Rene-Robert Cavelier, Sieur de La Salle, claimed the entire Mississippi Valley for France, calling the expansive area New France. The Mississippi Valley includes all of the land that became known as the Louisiana Territory, which stretched from the Mississippi River to the Rocky Mountains, and from the Canadian border to the Gulf of Mexico. Among the many present-day states in this large area are Illinois, Missouri, Minnesota, Iowa, Wisconsin, Arkansas, Kansas, Nebraska, and Colorado.

Thirty-two years later, a French officer and trader named Charles Charleville established a trading post at French Lick, which is near present-day Nashville. By the early 1750s, both Great Britain and France were competing with one another for control of the fur trade with the region's Native Americans. The British maintained good relations with the Cherokee and the Chickasaw, while the French remained close to the Creek.

In Europe, the French and the British had been warring with each other for decades. In 1754 that conflict spilled over into their land in North America. It became known as the French and Indian War because it not only involved France and Great Britain, but also Native American allies. In 1763, the war came to a close, and Great Britain, the victor, gained all of

France's land east of the Mississippi River. Now under British rule, the land that includes present-day Tennessee became part of the colony of North Carolina.

Early Settlement

After the French and Indian War, pioneers from Virginia, North Carolina, and Pennsylvania began making their way into the region that now includes Tennessee. A man named William Bean led one of these groups. In 1769, he and other North Carolinians established a settlement along the Watauga and Nolichucky Rivers. They built log cabins, each one a far distance from the other. To protect these far-flung dwellings from unfriendly Native Americans, they also built a fort.

In 1772 these same settlers established a system of self-government that was rare in North American colonies at that time. The system was called the Watauga Association. The settlers elected five magistrates, who made and carried out the settlement's laws. When the British colonial governor of North Carolina found out about the settlers' unique system of government, he was not pleased. He viewed it as a serious threat to his position, but he left it alone.

The Watauga Association was actually modeled after the constitution of the Iroquois League of Nations. This league was a system of self-government that five eastern Native American groups developed nearly two hundred years earlier.

Around the same time, another North Carolinian named Richard Henderson began to take an interest in the area now called Tennessee. He was a land speculator, which meant that he bought land in order to sell it at a higher price. Henderson hired a skilled woodsman named Daniel Boone to cut a trail from Virginia through the Cumberland Mountains into Kentucky. Boone finished the job, and the trail—which was called the Wilderness Trail—became the main route into the Tennessee area.

Once the trail was cut, Henderson wanted to make sure he controlled the land that surrounded it. So in 1775 he met with local Cherokee leaders at a place called Sycamore Shoals and struck a deal with them. In exchange for $50,000 worth of guns, ammunition, and other goods, the Cherokee gave Henderson and his Transylvania Land Company more than 20 million acres of land in both Tennessee and Kentucky.

Some of the Cherokee were angry about the deal. They felt they had been swindled. About a year later, under the leadership of a Native named Dragging Canoe, a band of Cherokee began attacking the Watauga settlements. Fighting stopped, however, in 1777 when the Cherokee warriors agreed to meet with representatives from North Carolina and Virginia. Peace was made and the Cherokee agreed to stay out of the war that the Virginia and North Carolina colonists were then fighting against Great Britain.

Now that peace with the Cherokee was secure, Henderson encouraged more and more settlers to move into the Tennessee region. Land around the Cumberland River was especially attractive. In 1779 he sold a huge part of it to a group of adventurous pioneers. After building their homes, they erected a fort on the banks of the Cumberland and named it Fort Nashborough. A few years later the settlement's name was changed to Nashville.

Spirit of Independence

At the same time Henderson was working on land deals with the local Native Americans, the Revolutionary War had begun. The thirteen colonies were fighting Great Britain to gain their independence. Because the frontier settlements of Tennessee were so far removed from the colonies, the area's settlers did not really pay that much attention to the struggle. However, when they found out that the British planned to take control of their territory, they quickly sprang to action.

On September 25, 1780, volunteers from Tennessee joined forces with more than 1,000 men from North Carolina and Virginia at Sycamore Shoals. Together the men set out on a journey to find Major Patrick Ferguson, the British military leader who was in charge of controlling Tennessee and the other "overmountain" territories.

One of Tennessee's nicknames is the Volunteer State. It received the name because of the courage displayed by its volunteer soldiers during the Revolutionary War and the War of 1812.

After a ten-day, 180-mile journey, the settlers, under the leadership of Colonel John Sevier of Watauga, caught up with Major Ferguson and his forces at Kings Mountain in South Carolina. The British forces were no match for the settlers, who were skilled in backwoods fighting methods. Firing their muskets from behind trees and bushes, the settlers won the battle easily after only an hour of fighting. The Battle of Kings Mountain marked a turning point in the Revolution in the south. The war officially ended when a peace treaty with Great Britain was signed in 1783. North Carolina—including its Tennessee territory—became part of a new nation called the United States of America.

Settlers cross the Cumberland River in search of new homes in unsettled land.

Fighting in the region still continued, however. Only this time it was with the Chickamauga, a renegade branch of Cherokee that continued to attack settlements in the Tennessee area. When Tennesseans turned to North Carolina for help in 1784, state government officials refused. They said it did not make sense to send the state militia to a territory that was so far away. To make matters worse, North Carolina gave control of the Tennessee territory to the United States government.

This angered the people living in the Tennessee territory. Representatives from three Tennessee counties met in Jonesboro to discuss the issue. After many debates, they drafted a constitution and formed their own state, which they named Franklin in honor of the patriot Benjamin Franklin. The settlers elected Colonel John Sevier—the hero of the Battle of Kings Mountain—as governor.

Unfortunately, Franklin collapsed four years later in 1788 when nobody ran against Sevier for the position of governor. Once again North Carolina assumed ownership of the Tennessee territory, but it did not last long. In 1790 the United States government declared Tennessee as the Southwest Territory. Knoxville became the capital.

The people of the Southwest Territory, however, noticed that other territories bordering the original thirteen colonies were becoming states. Vermont was admitted to the Union in 1791, followed by Kentucky in 1792. The people of the Southwest Territory wanted the same. So in January 1796, they petitioned for statehood. The federal government honored their request, and on June 1, 1796, Tennessee became the sixteenth state. John Sevier became the first governor.

Make a Herb Hot Pad

Tennessee settlers used a great variety of spices and herbs—
they learned about many of them from the Native Americans.
Some herbs were used for medicine or for cooking.
Others were used for their pleasant smells.
Following these instructions,
you can make a hot pad filled
with fragrant herbs. When you
place a warm bowl or dish on it,
the hot pad will release a pleasant
fragrance.

What You Need

2 square pieces of cotton fabric
    (9 inches by 9 inches)
Ruler
Pencil
Scissors
Sewing needle
Thread
1-1/2 cups dried herbs (you can use sage, bay
    leaf, lavender or just about any other nice-
    smelling herb.)

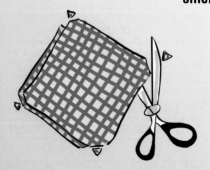

*Place the two pieces of fabric together. If
your fabric is printed or decorated, make sure
the printed sides of each piece are facing each
other.*

Using the scissors, cut off the four corners.

Use the needle and thread to stitch the two pieces together. Start your stitching about 1/4 inch from the edges of the fabric. If you need help, you can have an adult help you sew the fabric. Sew along all four sides of the square. Eventually you will be sewing toward where you first started the stitching. Leave a 2-inch gap between your last stitch and where you started sewing. Tie a double knot at the end of your last stitch.

Turn the fabric pouch inside out so that your stitching does not show. (If your fabric is printed, the printed side should be facing out.) Stuff the dried herbs through the 2-inch gap. Make sure the herbs are spread out pretty evenly throughout the pouch. Sew the 2-inch gap closed so that your pouch is sealed. Gently flatten out the pouch, and your hot pad is ready to use!

NOTE: Always check with an adult before putting anything warm on your hot pad. And never put a very hot pot, pan, plate, or cup on your hot pad.

A New State

In the first two decades after John Sevier became governor, settlers began pouring into East and Middle Tennessee through the Wilderness Trail. To make room for these settlers, in 1818 the federal government purchased a large amount of land from the Chickasaw in the west. It stretched from the Cumberland Valley all the way to the Mississippi River. In 1819 a port town was established on the Mississippi, and the settlers named it Memphis.

Nine years later there was a new president in the White House and his policies and beliefs would have a serious effect not only on the nation, but also on Tennessee. Andrew Jackson had lived in Tennessee and became a respected Nashville lawyer. He also served as a congressman and senator, and was a hero of the War of 1812. When he ran for the presidency in 1828, Jackson campaigned as a champion of the common man. He tried to demonstrate that even a person with humble beginnings could become president of the United States.

After Jackson won the election of 1828, he began to put his principles into practice. On a national level, he pushed for laws that would benefit ordinary people. With respect to Tennessee and the other states, he convinced Congress to pass the Internal Improvement Act of 1830, which set aside money to develop roads and rivers for transportation and trade purposes. For Tennessee's farmers, the legislation ensured they could get their crops to market more efficiently and cheaply.

Sadly, while addressing the needs of average white settlers, Jackson demonstrated no concern for Tennessee's Native Americans. At his insistence, in 1830 Congress passed the Indian Removal Act. The act called for the removal of the Cherokee people from their land in Tennessee to a designated area west of the Mississippi River. The Cherokee land in Tennessee was to be given to white settlements. So in 1838 federal troops rounded up 14,000 Cherokee men, women, and children and forced them to march more than 1,200 miles to a barren, deserted section of Oklahoma. With hardly any food and no warm clothes to protect them from the winter weather, more than 4,000 Natives died. The terrible journey is called the Trail of Tears.

Slavery and the Civil War

By the early to mid 1800s, slavery was becoming an issue in the country. The manufacturing-based states in the North were opposed to it. The southern states, on the other hand, felt it was necessary for their economy. Without slave labor they could

An illustration shows Memphis's busy port during the mid-1800s. Port cities like Memphis were important for shipping out crops from Tennessee's farms, and bringing in manufactured goods from other states.

not run their cotton plantations efficiently—and cotton production earned the plantations huge sums of money. For that reason, Southerners did not agree with the northern abolitionists who wanted to ban slavery forever.

In 1861 Abraham Lincoln became president. He strongly opposed slavery and wanted to stop it from spreading into the new western territories. The Southern slaveholders felt the decision on whether to be a free or slave state should be determined by each state, not by the federal government. The concept they championed became known as "states' rights." The slaveholders were also concerned Lincoln would restrict slavery in their own states.

In 1860 South Carolina seceded—or split—from the United States. Ten other Southern states followed, and together they formed the Confederate States of America, also known as the Confederacy. Tennessee, on the other hand, was reluctant to make such a move. In fact, many Tennesseans, including former President Andrew Jackson, were strongly in favor of preserving the nation.

However, things changed in April 1861 when Confederate forces bombarded Fort Sumter in Charleston, South Carolina. The Civil War had officially begun. Fearing an invasion from northern troops, Tennessee felt it had no other choice but to join its fellow Southern states. On June 8, 1861, Tennessee was the last Southern state to join the Confederacy.

During the Civil War, loyalties in Tennessee were largely divided. More than 135,000 Tennessee volunteers fought for the South. Nearly 70,000 Tennesseans—including 20,000 African Americans—served the Union. The majority of Tennessee's Union soldiers were from East Tennessee.

General Albert Sidney was the Confederate leader who was charged with defending Tennessee from Union forces, which were led by General Ulysses S. Grant. Grant's strategy was to control Tennessee's rivers and railroads. This would affect the state's main means of transporting and receiving goods, preventing supplies from reaching Confederate troops. In February 1862 Grant captured Fort Donelson on the Cumberland River and Fort Henry on the Tennessee River. Two months later he won the Battle of Shiloh in the town of Pittsburgh Landing near the Tennessee River.

During the Civil War more than 454 battles and skirmishes were fought on Tennessee soil. Virginia was the only other southern state to experience more military action during the war.

Union troops reclaim cannons and other weapons during the Battle of Shiloh.

The Battle of Shiloh was bloody for both the North and the South. General Johnston was killed during the battle. Historians estimate that more than 10,000 soldiers on each side were killed or wounded.

As more and more Tennessee towns began falling into Union hands, President Lincoln wanted to make sure Tennessee citizens obeyed Union laws. He appointed Andrew Johnson as military governor. Johnson was a former Tennessee governor who had remained loyal to the Union.

One of the turning points in favor of the North happened in June 1862 when Union forces captured Memphis. With that victory, the North had control of one of the South's leading cotton markets, as well as an important port on the Mississippi River. The Civil War finally came to an end in 1865 when General Lee surrendered in Virginia. Five days later, President Lincoln was assassinated while attending a play in Washington, D.C. Andrew Johnson, who had been elected to serve as his vice president, was now the new president. Johnson had the difficult job of rebuilding and healing a nation that had been torn apart by a major conflict.

Reconstruction and Recovery

When Andrew Johnson became president most members of Congress were in favor of punishing the Southern states that had rebelled against the Union. At first, Johnson felt the same way. But having grown up in Tennessee, he eventually began to feel differently. His heart went out to the people of his home state. Many of them had lost their businesses and farms because of the war. He proposed a more compassionate way for rebuilding Tennessee and other Southern states. This plan was called Reconstruction.

Reconstruction was made up of a variety of plans. One plan divided ten former Confederate states into five military districts. Each district was under the control of the United States military. Reconstruction also provided food, medical care, and resettlement plans for the newly freed African-American slaves.

In June 1865, two months after the treaty ending the Civil War was signed, Johnson drew up a plan to bring Tennessee back into the Union, and he presented it to Congress. But it took Congress nearly a year to even begin considering it. Finally on July 24, 1866, Tennessee became the first Southern state to rejoin the Union after approving two new amendments to the United States Constitution. These amendments ended slavery and extended the right to vote to all African-American men.

For the next few years, Congress continued to disagree with President Johnson over some of his Reconstruction plans. They felt he was not being harsh enough with the former Confederate states. Congress continued to pass tougher Reconstruction programs—despite the fact that Johnson disagreed with them. In one last attempt to heal old wounds and bring peace between the North and South, on Christmas Day 1868, Johnson issued a pardon to all former Confederate soldiers.

Some of Tennessee's African Americans were beginning to taste the benefits of their newly found freedom. In 1865 Congress established the Freedmen's Bureau, which set up seventy-five schools for blacks throughout the South. In 1866 the American Missionary Association founded the all-black Fisk University in Nashville. In addition, many African Americans began setting up their own businesses and running for public office.

But many whites did not like the political, economic, and educational progress some of Tennessee's African Americans were making. In 1866 in Pulaski, Tennessee, a former Confederate general named Nathan Bedford Forrest formed a secret society called the Ku Klux Klan. Its members wore white hoods and robes. In the evenings they would ride out on their horses, which were also covered with white sheets, and terrorize African Americans and their families. In many cases, they would even commit murder. In 1869 the state government of Tennessee passed a law that banned the Klan.

In 1872 a Nashville barber named Sampson W. Keeble became the first African American to serve in Tennessee's state legislature.

While it is true that some African Americans' lives improved, by the 1880s close to 90 percent of the African-American population in Tennessee were finding it very difficult to make ends meet. Many ended up working on the farms of their former slaveholders. They worked long hours and for very little money. Their landlords kept raising their rents, causing them to sink further and further into debt.

From the late 1870s and into the 1880s, the newly-gained rights of Tennessee's African Americans began to fade. For example, the state legislature passed a law requiring voters to pay a "poll tax." A poll tax is a sum of money voters pay the state for their right to vote. Many of the state's African Americans could barely afford to keep their families fed. Paying an additional tax—and for a right they had already been granted—was nearly impossible. In addition, some voters were required to take a literacy, or reading, test. If they did not pass, they could not vote. Since many African Americans had never gone to school, they often failed the tests.

Around the same time, a code of both written and unwritten laws also made their way into Tennessee and the other Southern states. They were called the Jim Crow Laws and they allowed discrimination against African Americans. African Americans had to ride in separate railroad cars and stay in separate hotels. In addition, they could not attend the same schools as whites.

Economically, Tennessee was in pretty good shape by the end of the nineteenth century. Its mining business in the southeast started to grow, as did manufacturing throughout the rest of the state. The wounds from the Civil War also showed signs of healing with the establishment of the Chickamauga and Chattanooga National Military Park in 1895. It is located in the same general area as the historic battles of Lookout Mountain, Missionary Ridge, Chickamauga, and Chattanooga. The park features monuments that honor both Confederate and Union soldiers who lost their lives during the war.

The Twentieth Century

By the twentieth century, Tennessee had made tremendous progress in terms of growth and opportunity. More and more towns and cities began building new schools. In addition, different products were being manufactured in the state. New factories specializing in the production of flour, paper, and cottonseed oil were built. The construction of new roads also made it easier for people to get back and forth to work and school, as well as to explore other areas of the state that may have been hard to reach in the past.

When the United States entered World War I in 1917, more than 100,000 Tennesseans joined the armed forces. In support of

Young girls work as knitters in a hosiery mill in Loudon around 1910.

the war effort, the state's factories became even busier, especially those involved in the production of cotton goods, clothing, aluminum, and ammunition for the troops overseas.

One of the great American heroes of World War I was Sergeant Alvin York of Pall Mall, Tennessee. For his bravery against the enemy, he was awarded the Congressional Medal of Honor—the United States military's highest honor.

Starting in 1929, Tennessee and the rest of the nation were hit hard by the Great Depression. Prices for manufactured goods and produce from the state's farms hit rock bottom. As a result, thousands of people lost their jobs. Farms and homes were lost. Many people had to move from their homes to find new jobs.

President Franklin Delano Roosevelt was concerned about the country's future. He helped to establish programs to create jobs for the people, while also improving the country. In 1933 the Tennessee Valley Authority—also known as the TVA—was created. The TVA was designed to control and direct the force of the Tennessee River to produce inexpensive electricity, to water crops, to improve river navigation, and to provide recreational facilities. It accomplished these goals through the construction of thirty-nine dams along the Tennessee River. In addition to creating hundreds of jobs for construction workers, the TVA, which was centered in Knoxville, also attracted many engineers and scientists to the state.

On the heels of recovering from the Great Depression, the United States entered World War II in 1941. Once again, thousands of Tennesseans volunteered for active duty. Approximately 200,000 citizens also worked in the state's war plants, turning out uniforms, aircraft parts, and other products for the military.

Workers build a new road in Lawrence County in the early 1930s. Projects such as these helped provide jobs for unemployed workers during the Great Depression.

In 1942 the federal government bought land on the Clinch River in Roane and Anderson Counties. An entire city, Oak Ridge, was built on this land. The government then attracted scientists, engineers, and other specialized workers to Oak Ridge by offering them housing and jobs. Some jobs at Oak Ridge included working with a radioactive element called uranium. This element was to be used in very powerful atomic bombs. Some of these bombs were dropped on Hiroshima and Nagasaki, Japan, abruptly ending World War II in August 1945.

President Franklin Roosevelt's secretary of state was Cordell Hull of Overton, Tennessee. Before he resigned from his post in 1944 because of poor health, Hull put together the plans that led to the formation of the United Nations (U.N.). The U.N. attempts to preserve peace through international cooperation, and to fight for human rights and the economic and social advancement of people all over the world. For this accomplishment and his efforts on behalf of world peace, Hull was awarded the Nobel Peace Prize in 1945.

Dreams and Promises

The 1950s marked a decade of great economic and social change for Tennessee. Many of the state's farmers began leaving their farms for other opportunities in Tennessee's larger towns and cities. With more people living and working in the cities, Tennessee grew into more of an industrial state as opposed to an agricultural one. As a result, the economy began to prosper.

Around the same time this was happening, the state's African Americans began to make progress in their fight against the Jim Crow Laws. In 1954 the U.S. Supreme Court—the highest court in the nation—ruled that separate schools for white children and black children were unequal, and, therefore, unlawful. The court ordered that black children be integrated, or admitted, into white schools immediately. Some black children were able to enter all-white

Though not all schools were integrated throughout Tennessee, some African Americans were able to attend schools with their white neighbors.

schools, but this was not true throughout the entire state. Many of Tennessee's white citizens were unhappy with the court's decision. As a result, there were a number of confrontations between whites and blacks—and some of these confrontations were violent.

During the 1960s, however, things began to change for the better thanks to the efforts of people like Dr. Martin Luther King Jr., a minister from Georgia. A very powerful speaker, Dr. King urged African Americans to have patience, commitment, and a spirit of non-violence in their quest for equal rights. Steady progress was made in ensuring equality for blacks not only in the nation's schools and universities, but also in the workplace. Sadly, on April 4, 1968, while in Memphis to address sanitation workers who were refusing to work because they wanted better benefits, Dr. King was assassinated. His legacy and influence lived on, however, as African Americans continued to make further progress in their peaceful battle for equal rights.

As Tennessee entered the twenty-first century, the state had grown economically, socially, and culturally. Manufacturing firms, attracted by Tennessee's location and skilled workforce, provided a variety of jobs. A steady stream of out-of-staters moving into Tennessee also contributed to a wider mix of different customs, traditions, ideas, and beliefs. In addition, the state grew more popular as more and more people began to explore—and then spread the word about—Tennessee's natural beauty, scenic parks, historical sites, and music scene.

Today Tennessee is a thriving state that has made significant advances in the areas of education and conservation. Its outstand-

ing colleges and universities continue to attract students from across the country and around the globe. In addition, between 1995 and 2000 the state reduced the amount of toxic chemicals it released into the environment. Throughout history, Tennesseans have worked to make their state the best it can be.

A view of the city of Gatlinburg. Today, most of Tennessee's residents live in or around the state's cities.

Important Dates

11,000 BCE Ancestors of today's Native Americans enter the region that includes Tennessee.

1673 James Needham and Gabriel Arthur travel through the region to develop the fur trade with Native Americans.

1714 Charles Charleville, a French officer and trader, establishes a trading post at French Lick, near present-day Nashville.

1763 The French and Indian War ends. Great Britain gains all of France's land east of the Mississippi River, including what would become the state of Tennessee.

1772 Tennessee settlers form the Watauga Association.

1784 Representatives from three Tennessee counties draft a constitution and form their own state named Franklin. John Sevier is elected governor.

1790 Tennessee becomes part of the Southwest Territory.

1796 Tennessee enters the Union as the sixteenth state.

1828 Andrew Jackson becomes the seventh president of the United States.

1830 President Jackson signs the Indian Removal Act, which forces the Cherokee to give up their lands in Tennessee.

1838 Federal troops round up approximately 14,000 Cherokee men, women, and children in Tennessee and force them to march more than 1,200 miles west to Oklahoma. The journey is known as the Trail of Tears.

1861 The Civil War begins and Tennessee breaks away from the Union.

1866 Tennessee is re-admitted into the Union.

1933 President Franklin Delano Roosevelt establishes the Tennessee Valley Authority (TVA).

1942 Oak Ridge is formed and becomes a center for industry and science.

1982 Knoxville hosts a world's fair.

2000 Tennessean senator Al Gore Jr. is nominated as the Democratic Party's candidate for president of the United States.

2004 Tennessee becomes the first state to establish anti-outsourcing legislation, which will help keep much-needed jobs in the United States.

John Sevier

Andrew Jackson

3 The People

After the end of the French and Indian Wars, British colonists from the Carolinas, Virginia, and Pennsylvania became very interested in Tennessee. They had heard of the state's lush meadows, rolling hills, and fertile lands. For them, this looked like a great opportunity. Within a few years, they began settling in Tennessee's Watauga River Valley and then in other parts of the region. These settlers were mostly colonists of Scottish-Irish descent. But there was also a number of settlers who could trace their ancestors back to Germany, Wales, and France. According to data gathered from the 2000 U.S. Census, Caucasians—or white people— now make up about 80 percent of the state's population. More than half of these residents are descendants of the state's original Scottish-Irish, English, German, Welsh, and French settlers.

When these European settlers came to the region hundreds of years ago—particularly those who settled in the

Tennesseans enjoy an amusement park ride.

Members of a bagpipe band in Nashville honor their European ancestry during a parade.

western section of Tennessee—they brought black slaves with them. The slaves worked in the region's cotton fields. By 1840 they numbered about 183,057. That was about a quarter of Tennessee's entire population at that time. There were also approximately 5,000 free blacks living in the state. After the Civil War ended, Tennessee's black population began to increase even more as freed slaves from Virginia, North Carolina, and South Carolina made their way into the state. However, possibly due to better job opportunities in other areas of the country, Tennessee's black population has declined during the past century. Today, African Americans make up about 16 percent of Tennessee's total population. The largest African-American populations in the state, are in and around Memphis.

Throughout the state's history, African Americans have helped to build, populate, and enhance many Tennessee communities. Several rural areas in Tennessee, small towns, and large cities are made up of hundreds of historical buildings that were designed and built by African Americans throughout the nineteenth and twentieth centuries. In fact, nearly every important late nineteenth- and early twentieth-century private and public building in Sevier County, which is located in East Tennessee, was constructed by black builders.

The cultural contributions that African Americans have made to Tennessee are also huge. In addition to introducing tasty foods that are well known today, they helped launch various musical styles. The roots of rock 'n' roll and the blues can be traced directly to Tennessee's African-American community in Memphis.

Other minorities make up smaller percentages of the population. Asians and Asian Americans represent only 1 percent of the state's population. People of Hispanic or Latino heritage make up a little bit more than 2 percent. The majority of Hispanics living in Tennessee are from Mexico (62.5 percent), Puerto Rico (8.3 percent), and Cuba (2.9 percent). They are Tennessee's fastest growing ethnic group. Between 1990 and 2000, the Hispanic population in

A trumpeter plays jazz on Beale Street in Memphis.

Nashville grew by 454 percent and in Memphis by 265 percent. Hispanics have been steadily moving into Memphis because of the increasing number of employment opportunities found in and around the city.

Tennessee's Asian Americans represent the state's second-fastest growing ethnic group, with an 86.1 percent growth in population between 1990 and 2000. The location of Japanese-owned automotive suppliers and other Asian-owned businesses near the state's larger cities like Memphis and Nashville have played a major role in this growth. Thriving communities and good schools have also drawn people from across the country and around the world.

Native Americans

Native Americans, Tennessee's original residents, represent less than 1 percent of the population. According to the 2000 U.S. Census, there are only about 17,068 Native Americans in Tennessee. The majority of these Native peoples are members of the Cherokee Nation. Their small numbers are the result of the United States government's land policies in the 1800s. Many Natives, such as the Cherokee, were forced to leave their ancestral homes to make room for white settlement. The Cherokee were moved to the barren plains of Oklahoma—more than 1,200 miles away. Though most Native American Tennesseans are Cherokee, some residents can trace their relatives to the Creek and Choctaw.

Like many Native Americans around the country, Tennessee's Native Americans are still struggling to earn the respect for their beliefs, customs, and traditions that they rightfully deserve. Fortunately, there are Native American

Cherokee dancers perform a traditional dance during a powwow.

organizations, such as the Alliance for Native American Indian Rights and the Native American Education Association. Their members in Tennessee work with government policy makers and legal experts to settle land disputes, as well as create and provide educational programs concerning Native American cultures.

Population Growth

According to the national census, in 1990 Tennessee's population was 4,877,185. By 2000 it had reached 5,689,283. That is a 16.7 percent rise, which is considered a large increase. What caused this growth?

More people both within the United States and from other countries have been attracted by the growth of jobs in the state, which began in the early 1980s. The auto industry,

Famous Tennesseans

Davy Crockett: Frontiersman, Soldier, and Politician

Born in Greene County, Tennessee in 1786, Crockett was a skilled hunter, woodsman, and scout. In 1823 he was elected to Tennessee's state legislature, and later he became a United States congressman. Crockett also wrote three books about his life experiences. He died at the siege of the Alamo in the war for Texas's independence.

Albert Gore Jr.:
United States Vice President

Albert Gore Jr. is the son of Albert Gore Sr., a U.S. senator from Tennessee. Like his father, Albert Gore Jr. was interested in politics. In 1976 he was elected to Congress and eventually became a senator. From 1992 to 2000, he served as vice president under President Bill Clinton. In 2000 Gore ran for president of the United States, but lost the election.

Aretha Franklin: Musician

Aretha Franklin started singing as a child with her sisters in their church. By the time she was fourteen, Franklin had already made her first recordings as a gospel artist. She became famous in the late 1960s with a string of fiery, emotion-charged songs such as "Respect," "Chain of Fools," "Baby I Love You," and "Think." Over the years, Aretha has earned the affectionate nickname "The First Lady of Soul."

Andrew Johnson: Politician and United States President

Johnson was born in 1808 in North Carolina, but as an adult, moved to Tennessee and opened a tailor shop. He later served as a Tennessee congressman and senator. In 1862 President Abraham Lincoln appointed him Military Governor of Tennessee. In 1864 he was elected Vice President of the United States. After Lincoln's assassination, Johnson became President and was faced with the difficult task of rebuilding a nation that had been torn apart by the Civil War.

Morgan Freeman: Actor

Born in Memphis in 1937, Freeman served in the Air Force before pursuing an acting career. Between 1971 and 1976 he played different parts on the PBS children's television series The Electric Company. *From the 1970s to present-day, Freeman has acted on stage, on television, and in the movies. He has been nominated for several acting awards, and recently won an Academy Award in 2005.*

Dolly Parton: Musician and Actress

Born in Sevierville, Parton started writing songs when she was only five years old. By the time she was thirteen, she was appearing on the Grand Ole Opry—*the longest continually running radio program in the United States. Within a few years, she became a successful singer-songwriter. Parton has starred in movies and on television. In 1985 she opened Dollywood, a theme park in the Great Smoky Mountains. Today, Parton continues to write music, sing, and participate in charitable causes.*

in particular, has grown tremendously. Tennessee's mild climate and relatively low cost of living have also drawn a lot of newcomers. Other people have come because of the state's beautiful scenery and warm, outgoing people

In 2000, 64 percent of Tennessee's population lived in the state's urban areas. The majority of these city dwellers lived in the suburbs of

Cities like Knoxville draw a number of different businesses and the people who run them.

My brother moved to Nashville in the mid-1980s and he couldn't stop talking about how friendly Tennesseans were. When my husband and I visited the state during one of our vacations, we experienced exactly what my brother was talking about. The people we met were absolutely wonderful and the scenery around the Great Smoky Mountains is incredible. We moved to Tennessee within a year of that visit.

— Martha McCann, a musician and resident of Nashville

Nashville, Knoxville, Memphis, Chattanooga, Clarksville, Johnson City, Jackson, and Murfreesboro. The remaining 36 percent lived in the state's rural settlements. These are mostly made up of small towns and farms.

Today—whether they live in large cities or small towns—Tennesseans are quick to point out that they are committed to improving the quality of living in their communities. A perfect example is the amount of money—half of it coming from taxes—which has gone into the state's school system. To date, Tennessee spends nearly $4,000 to educate each public school student every year. The good schools are just one of the many reasons why people make the Volunteer state their home.

Tennessee's rich cultural history, beautiful landscape, and great opportunities help to make the state a great place to live.

Calendar of Events

Eagle-watch Tours

As part of their migration south from the Great Lakes region and parts of Canada, bald eagles have chosen to spend their winters at Reelfoot Lake in the northwestern corner of Tennessee. These magnificent birds—with wingspans of 6 to 8 feet—can be observed in the wild at scenic Reelfoot Lake State Park as part of a tour program that begins in early January and ends the first week of March.

Dogwood Arts Festival

This festival, which takes place every April in Knoxville, highlights the city's dogwoods, azaleas, and other flowering plants that are in full bloom during the spring. The festival also includes plenty of arts, crafts, food, and entertainment by local artists.

West Tennessee Strawberry Festival

If you like festivals that celebrate small-town America, you should check out the West Tennessee Strawberry Festival, which occurs in Humboldt each May. The weeklong event includes parades, a carnival, street dancing, beauty pageants, and delicious West Tennessee strawberries.

The Rhododendron Festival

This festival, held at the foot of Roan Mountain the third or fourth weekend in June, pays tribute to one of Tennessee's most colorful wildflowers. The two-day event features handmade crafts, traditional mountain music, and old-time folkway demonstrations.

A bluegrass festival

State Fair

Since 1869 people from all over the state meet at this September event in Nashville. The fair includes all kinds of craft and agricultural displays and demonstrations, live entertainment, and a lot of food.

African-American Cultural Festival

This one-of-a-kind event, held in Chattanooga in September, showcases the state's rich African-American heritage in the areas of drama, dance, literature, and music. It also features a marketplace where visitors can shop for African-American clothing, food, jewelry, and crafts.

Asian Cultural Festival

In October visitors are invited to experience the cultures from the lands and nations of Asia with ethnic foods, traditional dances, and native music at the Asian Cultural Festival, which is held every October in Brentwood.

NAIA Powwow and Fall Festival

Each October in Nashville, Native Americans from around the country gather at this weekend festival to share parts of their culture. In addition to experiencing authentic Native food such as fry bread and hominy, visitors can also see Native American arts and crafts, jewelry, paintings, pottery, clothing, storytelling, and games.

Spinning wool at a fall festival

4 How It Works

Tennessee has 336 cities and towns. Each city and town has its own government—often a mayor and a council. These towns and cities are grouped together to form the state's ninety-five counties. Tennessee's local government operates mostly on the county level. An elected county executive is in charge of justices of the peace or magistrates who are elected by the citizens. As a group these officials get involved in managing elections, collecting taxes, settling wills, registering property titles, enforcing education laws, promoting library services, and other local duties. All ninety-five county executives meet with each other four times a year to discuss concerns and issues.

Tennessee's state government is divided into three parts: executive, legislative, and judicial. The governor heads the executive branch. The state's senators and representatives make up the legislative branch. The judicial branch is made up of judges who are in charge of the different state courts.

The state also has representatives at the national level. Tennessee voters elect two senators to serve six-year terms in Washington, D.C. Tennesseans also elect nine members of the

A Liberty Bell stands in front of the state capitol building in Nashville.

House of Representatives to serve two-year terms. These federal politicians represent Tennessee's interests and concerns regarding national issues.

Branches of Government

Executive Tennessee's executive branch makes sure that the state's laws are carried out. The head of the state's executive branch is the governor. He or she is elected to a four-year term by state voters. In addition to directing the laws passed by the legislature, the governor appoints the twenty-one members who make up the state's cabinet. Cabinet members help run the state.

Legislative Tennessee's legislative branch consists of a General Assembly. The Assembly is made up of a thirty-three-member senate and a ninety-nine-member house of representatives. Members of both houses are elected by citizens. However, those elected to the senate serve four-year terms, while those elected to the house of representatives serve two-year terms. Tennessee's General Assembly is responsible for passing and repealing—canceling—the state's laws. The branch also appoints Tennessee's secretary of state, state treasurer, and comptroller of the state treasury.

Judicial Tennessee's judicial branch interprets and applies the state's laws. The state's highest court is the supreme court. It is made of five members known as justices. Each justice serves an eight-year term and is elected by Tennesseans. The justices also elect one of their members to serve as chief justice. Tennessee's supreme court appoints an attorney general, who also serves an eight-year term. The judicial branch is also made of appellate courts and circuit courts, which are also known as trial courts. Municipal and county courts handle local issues and there are specialized courts that deal with juvenile issues and family matters.

How a Bill Becomes Law

Tennessee has a specific procedure for making laws. The ideas for laws can come from any resident of the state. Sometimes a resident suggests a law to the state senators or representatives, or the officials develop the idea on their own. The proposal for a law is called a bill.

The senator or representative proposing the bill gives it to the chief clerk. He or she examines the proposed bill to make sure it follows legislative rules. If it does, then the bill is given a number. According to Tennessee law, the bill then needs to be considered on three different days. The bill is first considered in the branch of the General Assembly where it was proposed. For example, if a state senator proposed the bill, then the state senate considers it first. If there is no objection to the bill on the first day of consideration, it is given to a standing committee on the second day. This committee is a group of legislators who have experience in certain areas. For example, a bill about the state's agriculture will be given to a committee of legislators who are familiar with agricultural issues and laws.

After the standing committee discusses the bill and its members recommend passing it, it is presented to the rest of the house or senate on the third day. At that time, the bill is open for debate and amendments—or changes—by the entire house or senate. After being examined and discussed, the bill may be passed with or without changes by a majority vote. A majority in Tennessee's house of representatives consists of fifty or more votes, while in the senate it is seventeen or more votes.

For hundreds of years, members of Tennessee's house of representatives have met and made laws in this room.

If the legislators vote in favor of passing the bill, it is sent to the other legislative house. There, the same three-day process takes place. If the proposed bill passes the second house, it is sent to the governor.

The governor may either sign the bill or veto—reject—it. He or she is allowed ten days to either approve or veto a bill. If the governor signs the bill it becomes law. A bill that is rejected by the governor can still be passed if a majority of both houses vote to override the veto. If no action is taken during that period, the bill becomes a law even without his or her signature.

If there is something you feel strongly about in your community or your state, try contacting your local legislators. Your government officials are there to help and represent you, and to make your state a better place to live. Together you can all make a difference.

To find contact information for Tennessee legislators go to this Web site:
http://www.tennesseeanytime.org/government/elected.html
You will need to know the name of your county or voting district. If you are not sure, ask a parent, teacher, or librarian to help you.

5   Making a Living

From the early eighteenth century until well into the twentieth century, Tennessee's economy was mostly based on agriculture. That began to change around the mid 1930s. Dams created by the Tennessee Valley Authority helped to harness the power of the Tennessee River. This created an inexpensive source of energy for factories. Manufacturing companies began moving to the region. In addition, an improvement in roads as well as methods of navigating the state's rivers and lakes made it easier for manufacturers to ship goods in and out of the state. Tennessee became more of an industrial state. Beginning in the 1980s, as more and more people began to move into Tennessee from other states, retail outlets, specialty shops, banks, and other service-oriented businesses started to increase.

Manufacturing

Manufacturing had a presence in Tennessee by the early nineteenth century, but the industry did not really begin to grow until after the TVA programs of the 1930s attracted many

The Nashville skyline at night.

companies. Today manufacturing makes up about 24 percent of Tennessee's gross state product, which is the total value of goods and services created by the state. The largest portion of that 24 percent comes from the production of automobiles and their parts.

Other manufactured goods that keep the state's economy moving at a brisk rate include plastics, rubber, metalworking machines, and construction equipment. Factories in the state also process foods and medication. Goods such as airplane parts, paint, soap, explosives, bicycles, paper, clothing, furniture, and surgical appliances and supplies are also manufactured in Tennessee's factories. These factories provide jobs for large numbers of residents.

A worker prepares to cut sheets of aluminum in a Tennessee factory. The aluminum will be used to make a variety of products.

Beginning in the 1980s, a number of high technology companies, including a few Japanese electronics firms, also moved into the state to set up production facilities. For that reason, Tennessee has been affectionately dubbed "the Silicon Valley of the South." ("The Silicon Valley" refers to a part of California that is known for its technology industry.)

Unfortunately, Tennessee's industrial boom has also affected the state in negative ways. Factories use or create a lot of chemicals and other substances during the manufacturing process. These chemicals and wastes are supposed to be removed in specific ways so that the surrounding environment

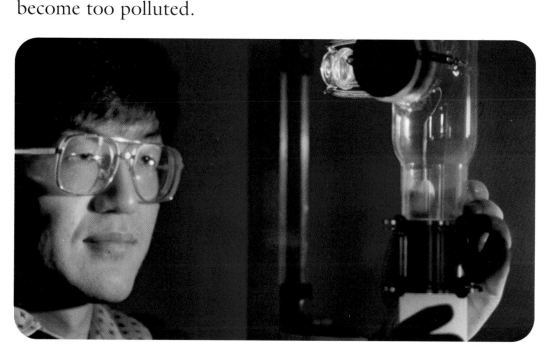

Gibson U.S.A., a world leader in the manufacturing of electric and acoustic guitars, is headquartered in Nashville. Among the many famous performing and recording artists who have used Gibson guitars are Keith Richards of the Rolling Stones, John Lennon of the Beatles, Elvis Presley, and Chuck Berry.

is not harmed. However, in 2004 it was discovered that the state had twelve hazardous waste sites—these are sites that have high amounts of dangerous waste. These sites were placed on a national list and are scheduled to be cleaned up. Residents who live near these sites are worried that the chemicals will enter the water and the land, killing plants and animals, and making people sick. The state has laws that require factories to properly dispose of their waste, and concerned citizens, business owners, and government officials are working together to make sure the state does not become too polluted.

Tennessee laboratories employ hundreds of research scientists across the state.

From the Earth

Although agriculture in Tennessee is not as widespread as it once was, it still plays an important role in the state's economy. As of 2003, Tennessee had approximately 87,000 farms that contributed about 1 percent of the total number of goods and services produced in the state.

This farm in Greenville grows tobacco, but also raises livestock such as cattle. Through the years Tennessee's agricultural industry slowed down as manufacturing and other industries gained popularity.

Each of the state's three regions—East, Middle, and West Tennessee—has a unique geographical make-up that plays a huge role in determining what is grown. For example, the fertile flatland areas of West Tennessee, enriched by silt flowing down from the Mississippi River, are perfect for growing cotton and soybeans. The area is also dotted with orchards that are well known for their peaches and apples.

Middle Tennessee, with its nutrient-rich soil and rolling hills, is ideal for raising beef and dairy cattle, as well as sheep. The green grassy fields are great for these grazing animals. Among the chief crops that are grown in this region, particularly in the Nashville Basin area, are wheat, potatoes, apples, and pears. The milder climate of East Tennessee is well suited for growing tobacco, snap beans, tomatoes, cabbage, and strawberries.

Recipe for Apple Crisp

West Tennessee is known for its orchards' rich apple harvests. Here is an easy-to-follow recipe for an apple treat that is bound to have your family members asking for seconds.

Ingredients:
1/2 cup of water
1- 1/2 to 2 teaspoons of cinnamon
4 cups of peeled apples
3/4 cup of flour
1 cup of sugar
1 stick of butter or margarine

Mix the water and cinnamon together in a bowl. Set the bowl aside while you peel and cut the apples. Have an adult help you cut the apples into slices. Place the apples in a baking dish and pour the cinnamon and water mixture over them.

Mix the flour, sugar, and butter or margarine with your hands until it is crumbly. Sprinkle the mixture over the top of the apples.

Bake the dish at 350 degrees for 1 to 1-1/2 hours. Keep an eye on the crumbly topping to make sure that it does not get burned.

When the topping is a golden brown color, have an adult help you remove the dish from the oven. Allow the dish to cool for about thirty minutes. You can serve the apple crisp cold, warmed up, or with a scoop of your favorite ice cream!

Tennessee also has a number of valuable minerals beneath its fertile soil. Some of the metals mined from the ground are copper, lead, manganese, iron, gold, and zinc. Tennessee is a leader in zinc production. The Knoxville area has the state's large zinc deposits. The zinc is mined and then shipped to factories where it is used in manufacturing.

The state's major non-metal mining products are limestone and coal. Crushed limestone is used in the manufacturing of concrete. It is also one of the ingredients used to pave roads. Tennessee's limestone deposits are concentrated in the eastern section of the state. Coal in Tennessee usually comes from the Appalachian Plateau, from underground and aboveground mines.

Service

A major part of Tennessee's labor force—about 33 percent—is involved in service industries. People who work in service industries provide a service to individuals or groups, as opposed to making a product or producing a crop. Examples of service industry workers include teachers, salesclerks, doctors, real estate agents, bankers, and musicians.

Most Tennesseans who work in the service industry are employed in the wholesale or retail trade. They can be found in grocery, clothing, greeting card, video, book, and music stores. The next largest group involves those who specialize in business, community, and personal services. Among these workers are doctors, nurses, legal assistants, teachers, and hotel clerks. The third-largest portion of the state's service employees work in finance, insurance, and real estate.

A service industry that has become associated with Nashville is the country music industry. This unique genre, or type, of music

The Grand Ole Opry is a favorite spot for tourists throughout the year.

was born in the mountains of eastern Tennessee in the late 1920s. A section of Nashville called Music Row is known the world over for its record companies, publishing houses, recording studios, and music clubs. Over the years, many country artists recorded their songs in Nashville, giving the city its nickname "Music City U.S.A." Their recordings and performances, including radio spots on Nashville's *Grand Ole Opry*, have made country music one of the most popular music styles in the country.

Another important service industry in Tennessee is tourism. This part of the service industry provides jobs for a countless number of Tennesseans. People who visit the state spend money on food, hotels, activities, and souvenirs. Tennessee businesses—and the state, as well—benefit from the money spent by tourists.

Tennessee's natural beauty attracts visitors throughout the year. People come to hike and camp in the wilderness areas, while others use the state's waterways for boating and swimming. Each year about nine million visitors travel to Great Smoky Mountains National Park in east Tennessee. The 521,000-acre park contains some of the most scenic areas in eastern North America. Its rolling streams, deep meadows, spectacular waterfalls, and majestic forests are a treat for residents and visitors alike.

For those who are interested in Tennessee's past, the state also has a variety of fascinating historical sites. One of the most

Products & Resources

Automobiles

Tennessee is a major player in the manufacturing of automobiles and automobile parts. General Motors—which is well known for its brand names such as Chevrolet, Pontiac, Cadillac, and Buick—has manufacturing facilities in the state. In addition, Japanese auto manufacturing companies have also opened plants in Tennessee.

Chemical Products

The Volunteer State plays a key role in the manufacture of chemical products. These chemicals are used to make things such as soap, paints, synthetic fibers, medicine, and explosive materials.

Cotton

For more than 200 years, cotton has played an important role in Tennessee's growth and development. According to historical records, 7,000 Tennessee acres were harvested for cotton in 1801. By 1821, that number had jumped to 130,000, making cotton among the state's chief cash crops. Today, close to one million bales of cotton are produced on 615,000 acres in Tennessee.

Limestone

Found in large amounts in the eastern part of the state, limestone is used for building roads and producing cement. Limestone is made up of layers of silt, small pieces of other rocks, and occasionally the skeletons of tiny creatures.

Baked Goods

The next time you are in your local grocery store and you notice a box of mouth-watering treats in the baked goods section, there is a pretty good chance they were packaged in Tennessee. Other baked goods that get packaged at Tennessee's packing facilities are cookies, brownies, cheesecakes, coffeecakes, and eclairs.

Country Music

Country music was born and bred in Tennessee's eastern mountains, so it is fitting that the state is a world-famous leader in the production, recording, and marketing of country music. Besides being the center of the country music recording industry, Tennessee also attracts tourists who are interested in hearing the music and seeing the country-music-related sites.

Part of Tennessee's tourism industry includes its amazing natural sites. Here, a visitor to the state enjoys the Ocoee River's white-water rapids.

popular is Chickamauga and Chattanooga National Military Park. Situated near Lookout Mountain—the site of an important Civil War battle in 1863—it is the largest and oldest military park in the United States.

Other popular tourist destinations in Tennessee are the Hermitage, which was President Andrew Jackson's home near Nashville, and Graceland, the mansion-like home of Elvis Presley, the "King of Rock and Roll." After the White House in Washington D.C., Graceland is the most frequently visited home in the United States.

Thanks to all of Tennessee's workers, the state has grown and prospered during the final decades of the twentieth century and into the twenty-first. The remote frontier outpost has been transformed into a bustling state that continues to attract visitors across the globe who are drawn to its natural beauty, fascinating history, and friendly people.

Tennessee's state flag depicts a red background with a blue band running vertically to the far right. Between the red background and the blue band is a thin white band. In the center of the red field is a blue sphere, whose outside is encircled by a thin white border. Within the blue spheres are three stars. These represent the state's three regions—East Tennessee, Middle Tennessee, and West Tennessee.

Tennessee's state seal is divided into two halves. The top half features images of a plow, a sheaf of wheat, and a cotton plant with the word AGRICULTURE inscribed beneath them. The bottom half features the picture of a riverboat with the word COMMERCE placed below it. There is a circular border around the seal, and it reads, "THE GREAT SEAL OF THE STATE OF TENNESSEE, 1796."

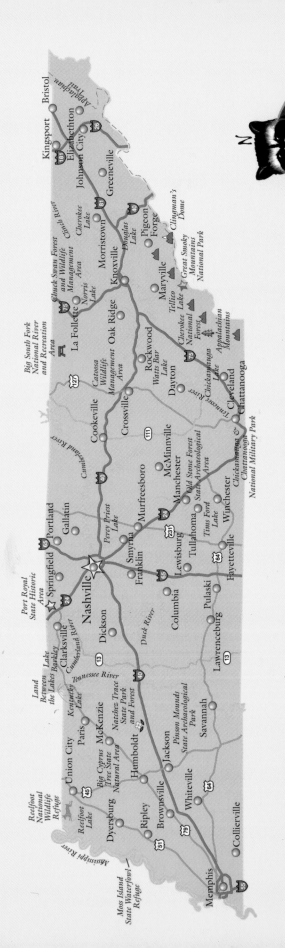

TENNESSEE

N E
W S

0 ___ 30
miles

Bristol
Kingsport
Elizabethton
Johnson City
Greeneville

Appalachian Trail

Cherokee
Lake
Morristown
Clinch River
Douglas
Lake
Pigeon
Forge
Clingman's
Dome
Great Smoky
Mountains
National Park

Chuck Swan Forest
and Wildlife
Management
Area
Norris
Lake
Knoxville
Maryville

Tellico
Lake
Cherokee
National
Forest
Appalachian
Mountains

Big South Fork
National River
and Recreation
Area
La Follette
Oak Ridge
Rockwood
Watts Bar
Lake
Dayton

Tennessee River
Chickamauga
Lake
Cleveland
Chattanooga

Catoosa
Wildlife
Management
Area
Crossville
McMinnville
Old Stone Forest
State Archaeological
Area
Chickamauga
Chattanooga
National Military Park

Cookeville

Cumberland River

Portland
Gallatin
Murfreesboro
Manchester
Winchester

Percy Priest
Lake
Smyrna
Franklin
Lewisburg
Tullahoma
Tims Ford
Lake
Fayetteville

Springfield
Nashville

Port Royal
State Historic
Area

Clarksville
Dickson
Columbia
Pulaski

Cumberland River
Duck River

Land
Between
the Lakes
Kentucky
Lake
Tennessee River
Paris
McKenzie
Natchez Trace
State Park
and Forest
Humboldt
Jackson
Pinson Mounds
State Archaeological
Park
Savannah
Lawrenceburg

Union City
Big Cypress
Tree State
Natural Area

Dyersburg
Ripley
Brownsville
Whiteville
Collierville

Reelfoot
National
Wildlife
Refuge
Reelfoot
Lake

Mississippi River

Moss Island
State Waterfowl
Refuge

Memphis

Legend

Interstate
Highway

U.S.
Highway

State
Highway

State
Capital

City or
Town

National
Forest

State Park

Wildlife
Refuge

Recreation
Area

Highest Point
in the State

Mountains

National
Park

Historic Area

Rocky Top

Words and Music by
Boudleaux Bryant and Felice Bryant

NOTE: *Tennessee has five different official state songs.*

More About Tennessee

Books

Ashby, Ruth. *The Diary of Sam Watkins, A Confederate Soldier.* New York: Benchmark Books, 2004.

Hawkes, Steve. *The Tennessee River.* Milwaukee, WI: Gareth Stevens, 2004.

Knapp, Ron. *Tennessee.* Berkeley Heights, NJ: MyReportLinks.com Books, 2003.

Web Sites

The Official Web Site of the State of Tennessee
http://www.tennessee.gov/

Tennessee Governor's Kids Page
http://www.tennessee.gov/governor/kids/index.html

Tennessee History for Kids
http://www.tnhistoryforkids.org/

Tennessee Travel and Tourism
http://www.tennesseeanytime.org/travel/index.html

About the Author

Rick Petreycik is a writer whose articles on history, music, film, and business have appeared in *American Legacy, Rolling Stone, Yankee, Disney Magazine,* and *The Hartford Courant,* among other publications. He lives in Connecticut with his wife, Pattilee, and daughter, Caitlin.

Index

Page numbers in **boldface** are illustrations.